Dedication

For our residents, whose stories inspire us every day,

and for their families and generations to come.

May the insights, memories, wisdom,

reflections and revelations recorded in these pages

be a source of delight to all who share it.

– Your Atria Family

You're

about to take an incredible journey.

Oh, the places you've been, the people you've known!

Life is filled with adventure, even if you never set foot outside your hometown.

You've experienced happiness, heartbreak, thrills, challenges and triumphs. Your journey is unique, your story is all your own. Only you are qualified to live your one amazing life – and to record your impressions of the way it happened.

Family and friends will cherish written memories of your life. So let's get rolling. We have a lot of ground to cover!

Bon voyage!

"When I was born
I was so surprised

I didn't talk for a year and a half."

Gracie Allen

"Would you like an adventure now, or shall we have our tea first?"

Peter Pan

SEE AMERICA

I came into this world:

(circle one)
at home / in a hospital or medical facility / in a taxicab / other: _____

_____

This is the story my family always told about the day I was born: _____

_____

_____

_____

My earliest memory is: _____

_____

_____

_____

_____

This lullaby was often sung to me: _____

_____

_____

When I was born...

...our family's primary mode of transportation was...

(please check)

☐ Automobile _____

                                    (what kind?)

☐ Bus

☐ Train

☐ Boat or ferry

☐ Bicycle

☐ Horse

☐ Feet

☐ Rickshaw

☐ Other: _____

...and we lived...

☐ In a house

   ☐ In a suburb

   ☐ In a city

   ☐ On a farm

   ☐ In a rural setting

   ☐ Other: _____

☐ In an apartment

   ☐ In a city

   ☐ In a suburb

   ☐ In a rural setting

   ☐ Other: _____

☐ In an igloo

☐ Other: _____

"IT AIN'T WHAT THEY CALL YOU,

My parents chose my name because: _____

_____

_____

_____

But, I wish they'd named me _____

instead because: _____

_____

_____

_____

I gained the nickname(s) _____

because: _____

_____

_____

_____

IT'S WHAT YOU ANSWER TO."

W.C. Fields

TOP **3** BABY NAMES

1930
Mary
Betty
Barbara
Robert
James
John

1950
Mary
Linda
Patricia
James
Michael
Robert

2014
Sophia
Emma
Olivia
Noah
Liam
Jacob

Source: United States Social Security Administration

Family Ties

The more we learn about our families the better we understand ourselves, our place in history and in the world. Recording your knowledge helps future generations hold on to pieces of their past.

_____ is the oldest relative I recall from my childhood.

This is what I remember about him/her: _____

_____

_____

_____

About my grandparents:

NAME	DATE OF BIRTH	PLACE OF BIRTH
MATERNAL		
Grandmother _____	_____	_____
Grandfather _____	_____	_____
PATERNAL		
Grandmother _____	_____	_____
Grandfather _____	_____	_____

These are some favorite memories of my grandparents: _____

_____

_____

_____

_____

About my parents:

	NAME	DATE OF BIRTH	PLACE OF BIRTH
Mother			
Father			

About my siblings:

NAME	DATE OF BIRTH	PLACE OF BIRTH

The traits I most admired about my mother are:

_____

_____

The traits I most admired about my father are:

_____

_____

The most important lesson(s) I learned from my parents:

_____

_____

_____

I regret not telling my parents this:

_____

_____

These words describe my relationship with my sibling(s):

_____

_____

My _____ was the primary disciplinarian of the family.

Historically, on Father's Day, more collect phone calls are made than on any other day of the year.*

*Source: AT&T

SAY, THAT REMINDS ME...

Use this space to jot down additional childhood memories.
Look through photographs, letters and other mementos to refresh your memory.

For example...

Who was your favorite teacher and why?

What was your favorite subject in school and why?

What games did you play at school?

READY, SET, GO – START WRITING!

"Adventure

can be an end in itself.

Self-discovery
is the secret ingredient. "

Grace Lichtenstein

I'm a custom-made model.

Each of us is an original. Every personality trait we have was either baked into our DNA from the beginning or learned along the way.

As you answer true or false to the items on the right, think about which traits you were born with and which you've picked up over the years.

True or False

I've always been more outgoing than shy............T/F

I'm a morning person..T/F

I consider myself photogenic............................T/F

I'm more street-smart than book smart............T/F

I love animals..T/F

I sunburn easily...T/F

People think I'm funny.......................................T/F

I'm good with numbers......................................T/F

I'm a decent cook..T/F

Babies are usually drawn to me.......................T/F

I have a good sense of direction......................T/F

I tend to walk faster than others......................T/F

I learned to juggle..T/F

I'm always cold..T/F

I've always napped easily.................................T/F

I have a decent singing voice..........................T/F

I'm ticklish...T/F

I enjoy dancing..T/F

I often get motion sickness while traveling..........T/F

I have at least one distinct mole or birthmark.....T/F

It is located on my _____

and looks something like _____

> # "Be yourself;
> ## everyone else is already taken."
>
> *Oscar Wilde*

(circle one)

I am left-handed / right-handed / ambidextrous

My favorite color is: _____

If I could only eat one food for the rest of my life, this is what it would be: _____
_____
_____

This is what I imagine people remember about me when I walk out of a room: _____
_____
_____
_____
_____

This is the trait I'm most glad I've passed down to my family: _____
_____

"It's always good to remember where you come from

and celebrate it."

Anthony Burgess

Base Camp

No matter how far we roam or how long we stay away, there's one place in the world we consider home.

Where's yours?

I spent most of my formative years in this place: _____

My family lived there because: _____

_____

These sights, scents and/or sounds always remind me of home: _____

_____

_____

_____

The names of our nearest neighbors were: _____

_____

Circle all that apply to the neighborhood, town, city or region you call your hometown:

Farmland	Suburban	Tropical	Arid	Unconventional	Backwoods
Rural	Friendly	Dry	Desert	Crowded	Gritty
Mountainous	Remote	Humid	Exciting	Sophisticated	Orderly
Seaside	Barren	Foggy	Peaceful	Noisy	Artistic
Urban	Lush	Forested	Traditional	Quiet	

" *When I was a kid, my parents moved a lot. But I always found them.* "

Rodney Dangerfield

LOCAL FLAVOR

The next time you eat lunch, think about this: potato chips are rumored to have been invented by a chef whose french fries were considered "too thick and soggy" by a complaining customer. Insulted and irritated, Chef George Crum of Moon's Lake House in Saratoga Springs, New York, retaliated by slicing potatoes extremely thin, then over-frying them to a crisp and dousing them with an abundance of salt before serving.

But what he intended to be a culinary insult turned into a customer favorite and Saratoga Chips (later known as potato chips) were born in 1853. Herman Lay later introduced them to the mass market and the rest, as they say, is history.

My hometown is famous for:

_____

_____

_____

_____

The best thing about where I grew up is:

_____

_____

_____

_____

A trip home isn't complete without:

_____

_____

_____

This famous person was born in my hometown:

_____

_____

"There are no foreign lands.

It is the traveler only who is foreign."

Robert Louis Stevenson

Where
in the
world
are **you**
from?

Many North Americans migrated here from someplace else, at some point in time.

What are your family's unique origins?

My ancestors came from the following countries:

Mother's side: _____

_____

Father's side: _____

_____

These relatives spoke in another language around the family: _____

_____

These special celebrations or customs were passed down to my family: _____

_____

_____

Many people in my family share this characteristic: _____

_____

_____

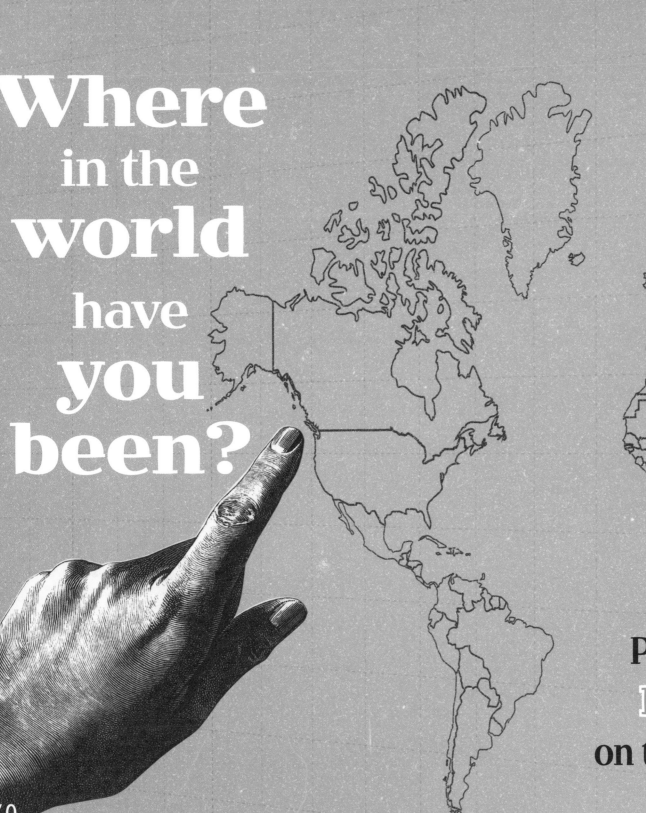

Where
in the
world
have
you
been?

Put your mark on the map!

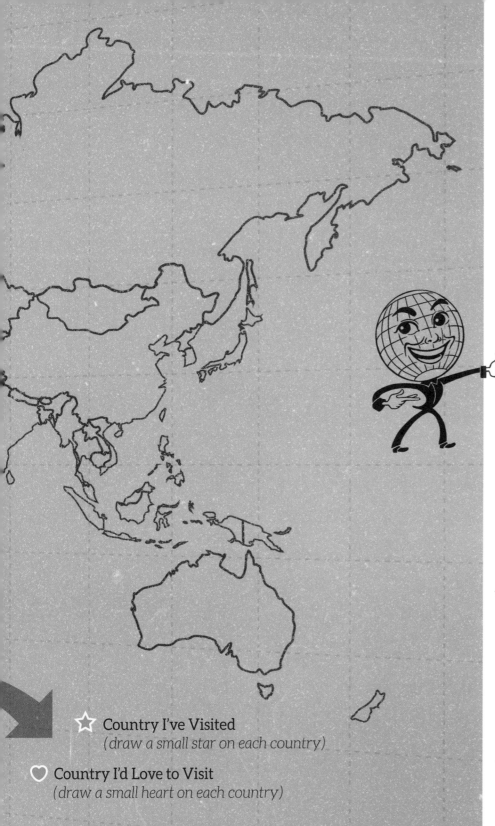

If I could travel anyplace in the world it would be:

_____

Here's why: _____

_____

_____

My favorite place I've ever traveled to is:

_____

Here's why: _____

_____

_____

Regardless of where I've lived, the ideal environment for me is:

☐ A beach

☐ The mountains

☐ Grassy prairie

☐ The desert

☐ The forest

☐ Other: _____

☆ Country I've Visited
(draw a small star on each country)

♡ Country I'd Love to Visit
(draw a small heart on each country)

"Their story, yours and mine – it's what we all carry with us on this trip we take,

and we owe it to each other
to respect our stories
and learn from them. "

William Carlos Williams

Around the
Campfire

This story was told to me by my mother.

Every spring, my grandfather had a ritual; he would simmer a big pot of "tonic" on the stove and then try to persuade my mother and her three sisters to drink a cup, which, with crinkled noses, they staunchly refused to do year after year.

Raised on a farm in the west of Ireland, my grandfather immigrated to the United States in the 1920s. Always health conscious, he claimed his tonic – most likely made of nettles and other wild greens – cleansed the blood and rid it of the toxins built up over the winter. Speaking with a thick, often indecipherable brogue, his motto was "You can spend your money at the grocer's or at the doctor's office. Your decision."

Turns out, Grandpa was on to something; nettle tonics have been used for centuries around the world, and today the sticky green plant is considered a "super food" rich in nutrients and antioxidants.

Simple stories like this help us understand our families and where we ultimately came from. Personal folklore is family gold and deserves to be treasured as such.

Every family has a history, a collection of stories and anecdotes, starring characters large and small, infamous and illustrious, unforgettable or slowly fading from view.

With each passing year, it becomes increasingly vital to record your family's stories for future generations.

What stories can you share?

Here's a story involving one of the more colorful characters in our family:

_____

_____

_____

_____

_____

_____

These expressions are widely used in my family:

_____

_____

_____

_____

_____

This story is about a holiday gone wrong:

_____

_____

_____

_____

_____

The best love story in my family is:

_____

_____

_____

This family tidbit belongs in the "skeletons-in-the-closet" category:

_____

_____

_____

_____

This is a story about how my family got through hard times:

_____

_____

_____

_____

To help stretch every dollar, my mother and father did the following:

_____

_____

_____

As a result, I picked up the following habits:

_____

_____

Use this space to record more family stories.

For example...

What dishes or recipes have been passed down
in your family and where did they originate?

What professions or careers are common in your family?

What was the best advice you ever received from a relative?

_____

_____

_____

_____

_____

_____

_____

_____

_____

For fun...

Ask a friend or family member to write down your stories as you
tell them, or use a video camera or other recording device to help
with the process and write your stories down on paper later.

_____

_____

_____

_____

_____

_____

_____

_____

_____

_____

_____

_____

_____

_____

" *Another belief of mine; that everyone else my age is an adult, whereas I am merely in disguise.* **"**

Margaret Atwood

"It must be wonderful to be seventeen,

and to know everything."

Arthur C. Clarke

SETTING YOUR COURSE

Growing up.
Getting older.
Hopeful.
Fearless.
Impatient.
Determined to stand
on your own two feet
and make your place
in the world.

When I grew up, I wanted to become a: _____

because: _____

_____

_____

The adult I admired most in my teens was: _____

because: _____

_____

_____

The highest grade I completed was: _____

I attended high school at: _____

and participated in these school activities and sports: _____

_____

_____

These additional hobbies, chores or jobs kept me busy after school: _____

_____

_____

Following high school, I attended this college and post-secondary school: _____

_____

_____

Postcards from the Past

Memories are often brief anecdotes, fleeting moments – snapshots of everyday life. Time covers them with a poignant patina.

Depending on what year and where you were born, some of the following reminiscences may sound familiar. Share your own memories below.

_____

_____

_____

_____

_____

_____

_____

_____

_____

_____

_____

_____

_____

"As a little girl I remember vegetables and other goods being sold from a horse-drawn cart and dinner on Sundays with my grandparents." *Gloria*

"To help in the war effort, we brought certain materials to school on Friday afternoons: metal, rubber, glass, fat, paper and other things. Mother also had to go to the school at intervals to collect our ration books. Everyone had to have a ration book – even babies and young children." *Norma*

"Letters were important. Our mailbox was always full. People wrote letters every week, even every day. I wrote to soldiers overseas. Also, pen pals were a big thing. I had one in Australia, a girl named Eunice. There was no TV; we would get pictures of the war in Europe on the newsreel at the movie theater." *Inie*

"Whenever I announced I had a sore throat or cough, my mother would soak a rag in coal oil and wrap it around my neck at bedtime. The symptoms were usually gone by morning." *Neal*

"We didn't have running water. We carried it in buckets from an outside well. Hot water heaters were almost unheard of; water was heated on top of the stove (ours was wood burning) and used for washing dishes, clothes and bathing. Needless to say, baths were weekly, not daily like today." *Sondra*

"What I recall most strongly was war savings stamps, and having those poor Dionne Quintuplets paraded at a war bond drive. And sending cigarettes overseas whenever finances permitted." *Flora*

"Morale is a woman's business

…it's a woman's duty to keep beautiful even in the rush of war days. Psychologists say the way women look affects the entire community, not only civilians but the outlook of the men in the armed forces…"

Excerpted from "The Wartime Home-Maker: A Little Magazine of Interest to Women" published in Saint John, New Brunswick, Canada.

The wars I've lived through are: _____

The most significant effect war has had on my life was: _____

_____

_____

_____

The memory of how my family contributed to the war effort is: _____

_____

_____

_____

If there was one lesson I want future generations to know: _____

_____

_____

_____

"Use what talents you possess.

The woods would be silent if no birds sang except those that sang best. **"**

Henry van Dyke

THE 7 WONDERS OF YOU

Here are 7 achievements I'm most proud of:

1 _____

2 _____

3 _____

4 _____

5 _____

6 _____

7 _____

Here are 7 things I've received compliments on:

1 _____

2 _____

3 _____

4 _____

5 _____

6 _____

7 _____

I have a natural talent for: _____

_____

_____

And I've put it to use by: _____

_____

_____

> " *I think that the most important thing a woman can have – next to talent, of course – is her hairdresser.* "
>
> Joan Crawford

"Today was good.
Today was fun.

Tomorrow is another one."

Dr. Seuss

ROADSIDE ATTRACTIONS

During long trips, it's important to occasionally pull over, turn off the engine, step out of the car, stretch your legs and enjoy the scenery.

How fun am I?

TAKE THIS QUIZ AND FIND OUT!

SCORING:

1 POINT each **C** answer

2 POINTS each **B** answer

3 POINTS each **A** answer

Total your score. The higher the score, the more fun you are!

What can you do this week to make life more fun?

If a friend suggested a new and daring (but safe and legal) activity, I would:

A. Try anything once – twice if I like it!

B. Mull it over and decide later

C. Politely decline. Better safe than sorry!

The last time I acted spontaneously was:

A. This week

B. This month

C. Longer ago than I remember!

Most of my friends are:

A. Unpredictable and spontaneous

B. Easygoing, happy-go-lucky

C. Sensible and down to earth

Silly or serious – I am more:

A. Silly

B. A little of both

C. Serious

Amongst my friends:

A. I am the one who persuades them to be adventurous

B. They're the ones who persuade me to be adventurous

C. They try to persuade me to be adventurous, but almost always fail

"Imagination is everything. It is the preview of life's coming attractions."

Albert Einstein

Pit Stop for Playtime

Being an adult is serious business.

However, in his book titled *Play*, Dr. Stuart Brown makes a strong case for goofing off. He's discovered that pure, aimless frivolity can boost problem solving, creativity, intimacy with strangers, strengthen established relationships and cultivate physical healing.

Play can involve art, music, singing, dancing, etc. But it's important to remember that play is not a specific "thing" or goal to achieve. By nature, it is a state of being that's purposeless, with no objective other than 100 percent enjoyment.

Silly Stories

Grab a partner and fill in the blanks, asking them for only the kind of word indicated beneath each blank. Do not show your partner the story in progress. Once completed, you can read the story aloud!

The Very _____ Day, by _____
                (adjective)   (respondent's name)

_____'s day began as usual, with a big cup of _____
(woman's first name)   (liquid beverage)

and a healthy serving of _____. Despite her comforting routine,
                          (type of food)

_____ felt _____, as if something
(woman's name)   (an emotion)

_____ might happen that day. After a few moments she thought,
(adjective)

"_____! I'm probably just _____ things!"
(exclamation)   (verb ending in "-ing")

But just outside her door, _____ discovered a _____
                          (same woman's name)   (noun)

most likely left behind by a _____.
                          (type of animal)

"_____," she cried out loud. Maybe this day would turn out
(exclamation)

_____ after all!
(adjective)

"Saving the world is only a hobby.

Most of the time I do nothing."

Edward Abbey

> **Fall in love with as many things as possible.**
>
> Unknown

My favorite hobbies, interests and passions have been:

(circle all that apply)

Antiquing

Travel

Camping

Politics

Physical fitness

Spiritual faith

Volunteering

Movies

Reading books

Knitting

Embroidery/Needlework

Crafting

Fishing

Bowling

Crossword puzzles

Running

Cycling

Card games

Listening to music

Meditation

Boxing

Chess

Performing arts patron

Watching sports

Scrapbooking

Gardening

Collecting _____

Woodworking

Cooking/Baking

Sewing

Hiking/Nature walking

Painting/Drawing

Photography

Building model _____

Origami

Glassblowing

Weaving

Sculpture

Golf

Tennis

Racquetball

Pottery/Ceramics

Acting/Theater

Singing

Poetry

Playing _____
(musical instrument)

Horse riding

Hunting

Bird watching

Scuba diving

Swimming

Dog breeding

Quilting

Wine tasting

Home canning and jarring

Jewelry making

Skiing

Rafting/Canoeing

Sailing

Dancing

Yoga

Writing _____

Genealogy

Magic tricks

Floral arranging

Table tennis

Martial arts

Other: _____

"Know the rules well,

so you can break them effectively. **"**

Dalai Lama XIV

Rules of the Road

Growing up, the following landed me in hot water with my parents:

(check all that apply)

- ☐ Smoking cigarettes
- ☐ Drinking alcohol
- ☐ Cursing
- ☐ Skipping school
- ☐ Skipping church
- ☐ Stealing
- ☐ Being caught at home alone with a member of the opposite sex

- ☐ Driving without a license
- ☐ Receiving an "F" or failing score on a test or report card
- ☐ "Talking back" or "sassing" my parents
- ☐ Caught telling a lie
- ☐ Disrespecting an adult

Other: _____

_____

This is how I think disciplining children today differs from when I was a child:

_____

_____

_____

_____

_____

_____

_____

A butcher *who'd had a particularly good day, happily flipped his last chicken on a scale and weighed it. "That will be $6.35," he told his customer.*

"That's a good price, but it's a little too small," the woman replied. "Do you have anything larger?"

Thinking fast, the butcher returned the chicken to the refrigerator, paused a moment, then took the same chicken out again.

"This one," he said as casually as possible, "will be $6.65."

The woman paused for a moment, then made her decision.

"You know what?" she said, "I'll take them both!"

At some point in my life, I did the following without suffering consequences or getting caught, and then felt remorseful afterward:

(check all that apply)

☐ Stole money

☐ Shoplifted

☐ Cheated on a test

☐ Told a big lie

☐ Openly ridiculed someone

☐ Spread a rumor

☐ Took credit for something I didn't do

☐ Other: _____

_____

_____

_____

_____

This is why I felt bad:

_____

_____

_____

This is what I did about it:

_____

_____

_____

And this is what I learned from that experience:

_____

_____

_____

The first significant argument or disagreement I was ever involved in was about:

_____

_____

_____

_____

_____

" *Integrity is doing the right thing even when no one is watching.* "

C. S. Lewis

"A SMOOTH SEA

NEVER MADE A SKILLED SAILOR."

English proverb

WHEN THE GOING
GETS TOUGH

Hardship is a part of life. It creates resiliency by giving us opportunities to learn from experience and choose to rise above it.

How has adversity shaped your life?

When something bad happens, this is how I cope:

_____

_____

_____

_____

This unpleasant event taught me one of the most important lessons of my life:

_____

_____

_____

_____

My advice to others faced with misfortune is:

_____

_____

_____

_____

> **" Some beautiful paths can't be discovered without getting lost. "**
>
> *Erol Ozan*

"Parents can only give good advice or put them on the right paths,

but the final forming
of a person's character
lies in their own hands."

Anne Frank

YOUR
TRUE
NORTH

My top values right now are:

(circle all that apply)

Family	Belief in others
Friends	Respect
Kindness	Cooperation
Financial security	Work/industriousness
Beauty	Nature
Creative expression	Spirituality
Adventure/experiences	Trust
Knowledge/wisdom	Integrity
Helping others	Dedication
Achievement	Forgiveness
Optimism	Honesty
Gratitude	Love
Tenacity	Patience
Faith	Generosity
Social standing	Other: _____
Recognition	_____
Physical health/fitness	_____
Compassion	_____
Tolerance	_____

Each of us navigate the world using our own moral compass and map of core values.

What do you value most?
What beliefs and morals guide you?

At age 18, my top values were:

_____

_____

_____

At age 35, my top values were:

_____

_____

_____

At age 65, my top values were:

_____

_____

_____

At age 100, I think my values will be:

_____

_____

_____

This person influenced my values and beliefs and here's how:

_____

_____

_____

_____

When I'm feeling uncertain about something, I imagine what

_____ would do in the same situation.

These are the values I hope I've instilled in my family and here's why:

_____

_____

_____

_____

_____

_____

If I were granted three wishes for the world today, this is what I would choose and why:

WISH **1**
_____
_____
_____
_____

WISH **2**
_____
_____

WISH **3**
_____
_____
_____

"There is unmapped territory

in all of us. **"**

Anonymous

What drives you?

Do you have passion? Energy? Ideas?

You need the right fuel – both physically and philosophically – to keep your motor humming along at a meaningful pace. You need a dream, a goal or a mission, no matter how small or large.

Want to plant a few rose bushes to brighten up a grey corner outdoors? Write your first novel? Visit Japan? Get a tattoo?

Do it.

My passion is:

_____

_____

_____

_____

This is how I'm sharing that passion with others:

_____

_____

_____

If you think you're too old for dreams, remember...

Your model year doesn't matter.

At age...

62 *Colonel Sanders founded Kentucky Fried Chicken*

65 *Laura Ingalls Wilder published the first book in her beloved "Little House on the Prairie" series*

70 *Golda Meir was elected fourth Prime Minister of Israel*

75 *Grandma Moses began painting, eventually reaching worldwide fame for her art*

92 *Gladys Burrill becomes oldest woman ever to finish the Boston Marathon*

103 *A practicing pediatrician her entire life, Dr. Leila Denmark finally retires*

"A ship is safe in the harbor,

but that's not what
ships are built for. "

Gael Attal

Give it a Spin

When was the last time you tried something new?

Here's a list to inspire you. Feel free to invent your own pursuit. But choose one and make it a priority this week:

- Learn to say "I love you" in a new language

- Try a unique hair color

- Paint your toenails a crazy shade

- Say "yes" to every invitation or request for one full day

- Choose a new hobby such as scrapbooking or bird watching and practice it once a week

- Learn a new joke and tell it throughout the week

- Give five genuine compliments to five different people

- Perform a random, secret act of kindness

Here's something I didn't want to try, but ended up liking:

_____

_____

_____

_____

This is something I've always wanted to do but haven't...*yet*:

_____

_____

_____

_____

_____

_____

" *Without new experiences, something inside of us sleeps. The sleeper must awaken.* "

Frank Herbert

"Love is that condition in which the happiness of another person *is essential to your own.*"

Robert A. Heinlein

My Better Half

I met my spouse: _____

_____

_____

The first thing I liked about him/her was: _____

_____

_____

I knew he/she was "the one" when: _____

_____

_____

_____

Our marriage proposal happened this way: _____

_____

_____

Our wedding took place on: _____ at _____
                              (date)   (place)

My favorite memory of that day was: _____

_____

_____

> ❝ *Nobody has ever measured, not even poets,*
> *how much the heart can hold.* ❞
>
> Zelda Fitzgerald

"Cleaning your house while your kids are still growing is like

shoveling the sidewalk
before it stops snowing. "

Phyllis Diller

Little Rascals

About my children:

NAME	DATE OF BIRTH	PLACE OF BIRTH

This is how I learned I would be a parent for the first time: _____

_____

_____

This is how I felt: _____

_____

_____

The first person I shared the news with was: _____

Talking About Your Generation

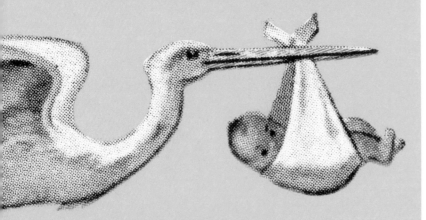

When we're born can have a lot to do with what kind of people we grow up to be. Today, six socially and demographically defined generations are sharing the planet at the same time.*

*Source: Pew Research Center

The Greatest Generation: born 1900 to 1936

General Qualities: resilient, resourceful, frugal

Influential Experiences: World War I, Jazz Age, The Great Depression, World War II

The Silent Generation: born 1937 to 1945

General Qualities: ambitious, traditional, loyal

Influential Experiences: The New Deal, Korean War, television

Baby Boomers: born 1946 to 1964

General Qualities: idealistic, rebellious, innovative

Influential Experiences: civil rights, Kennedy and King assassinations, Vietnam War, first moon landing

Generation X: born 1965 to 1976

General Qualities: independent, self-reliant, balanced

Influential Experiences: Desert Storm, AIDS, home computers, video games

Millennials: born 1977 to 1990

General Qualities: confident, optimistic, inclusive

Influential Experiences: September 11 attacks, Iraq War, Internet, cell phones

Internet Generation: born 1996 to 2010

General Qualities: self-directed, multitasking, team-oriented

Influential Experiences: Social media, The Great Recession, smartphones

Becoming a parent changed the way I looked at life in this way: _____

_____

_____

_____

_____

_____

My best advice about raising children is: _____

_____

_____

_____

_____

_____

The funniest thing my child ever did or said was: _____

_____

_____

_____

" *A child is a curly, dimpled lunatic.* "

Ralph Waldo Emerson

"It's the friends you can call up at

4 a.m.
that matter. "

Marlene Dietrich

The Best Mirror is an Old Friend

My longest friendship has been with: _____

We met at: _____ when I was _____ years old.

This is how we became friends: _____

_____

_____

_____

_____

No matter what, I could always depend on the following friend to help me in a time of need: _____

_____

The friend I've most admired was _____ and this is what I admired about him / her:

_____

_____

_____

The newest friend I've made is _____ and this is how we met: _____

_____

_____

"My socks may not match,

but my feet are always warm. "

Maureen McCullough

My Attitude of Gratitude

When we take the time to look around,
we can find plenty to be thankful for.

Throughout my life, including today, these are the people I'm most grateful to have known:

1 _____
2 _____
3 _____
4 _____
5 _____
6 _____
7 _____
8 _____
9 _____
10 _____

In addition to friends and family, I am also thankful for:

1 _____
2 _____
3 _____
4 _____
5 _____
6 _____
7 _____
8 _____
9 _____
10 _____

A man pulled into a gas station and asked the attendant

"What are the people like in the next town up ahead?"

The employee replied, "What were the people like in the town you just came from?"

"Awful people," the man responded. "Rude, cold, hostile, abrupt, unfriendly. They wouldn't give me the time of day."

"Well," said the attendant, "I'm sorry to say it, but you're going to find exactly the same sort of people in the next town up ahead."

A bit later, another driver pulled in, heading in the same direction as the first. "What are the people like in the next town up ahead?" the second man asked. The attendant said, "What were the people like in the town you just came from?"

"Wonderful people," the second man responded. "Friendly, warm, helpful, patient, kind. They went out of their way to help a stranger."

"Well," said the attendant, "I'm happy to tell you that you're going to find exactly the same kind of people in the next town up ahead."

"We are not human beings having a spiritual experience.

We are
spiritual beings
having a
human experience.**"**

Pierre Teilhard de Chardin

I believe...

This is how and when I found my faith:

_____

_____

_____

_____

_____

_____

This is how I put my beliefs into practice:

_____

_____

_____

_____

_____

_____

_____

> " _Our idea of God tells us more about ourselves than about Him._ "
>
> Thomas Merton

Here is how faith has influenced my family life: _____

_____

_____

_____

_____

My faith was tested most when: _____

_____

_____

_____

_____

When I die, I believe this is what will happen: _____

_____

_____

_____

_____

" *Faith is not something to grasp, it is a state to grow into.* "

Mahatma Gandhi

"HISTORY
NEVER LOOKS LIKE

HISTORY

WHEN YOU ARE LIVING THROUGH IT. "

John W. Gardner

CHANGING
DIRECTIONS

One thing in life is certain: change. What marvelous transformations have you witnessed?

In my lifetime, I think these inventions have altered society the most:

_____

_____

_____

_____

Here's how:

_____

_____

_____

_____

The change I've witnessed in the world that most concerns me today is:

_____

_____

_____

_____

Here's why:

_____

_____

_____

_____

AND ANOTHER THING...

Use this space to elaborate further on how certain things have changed over your lifetime, and whether you think it's positive or negative.

For example:

How has the role of women evolved over your lifetime?

How have people's attitudes about their health changed?

Is the food we eat today better or worse than when you were younger?

What's different about the way people dress out in public?

In the span of 66 years, we went from our first flight in an airplane to our first rocket landing on the moon.

" **NO ONE CAN POSSIBLY KNOW WHAT IS ABOUT TO HAPPEN:**

IT IS HAPPENING,
EACH TIME,
FOR THE FIRST TIME,
FOR THE ONLY TIME. **"**

James Arthur Baldwin

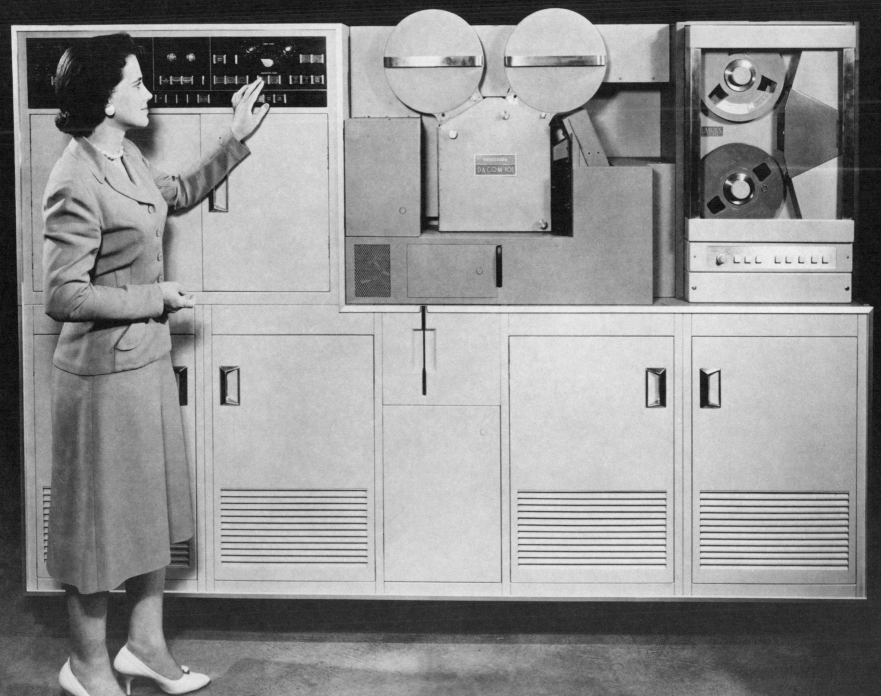

The first movie I ever saw in a theater was:

_____

I was _____ years old the first time I saw a TV.

Gasoline was _____ per _____
when I first started driving.

I was _____ years old the first time I spent an
extended period of time away from home.

This is where I went and why:

_____

_____

_____

My first home away from my parents' home was:

_____

The first big thing I saved my own money to purchase was:

_____

_____

The first person who broke my heart was:

_____

My first pet was a _____

named _____

The first thing people tend to notice about me is:

_____

_____

_____

The first time I drank too much alcohol, this is what happened:

_____

_____

_____

The first time I flew in an airplane:

My age: _____

My destination:

_____

My level of fear:

_____

My first kiss was *(select all that apply)*

☐ Awkward   ☐ Romantic

☐ Sweet   ☐ Disappointing

☐ Accidental   ☐ Thrilling

Ancient Sumerians are thought to have been the first people to keep written records. Clay tablets from 3000 B.C. and earlier have been found containing records of business transactions and judgments.

"**Not everything worth keeping**

has to be useful. ''

Cynthia Lord

Souvenirs from the Road

Along the way, we pick up some material possessions that take on extra meaning because they remind us of special people, places or experiences.

In fact, the English translation of the French word *souvenir* is memory.

If I could travel back in time, I would retrieve _____ from my childhood.

If my home caught fire and I could save only one item, this is what it would be and why:

_____

_____

_____

_____

My family's most treasured heirloom is: _____

because: _____

_____

_____

My favorite childhood birthday or holiday gift was:

_____

_____

_____

_____

" Yesterday is history, tomorrow is a mystery,

**but today is a gift.
That's why we call it the present.** "

A. A. Milne

Today
is the Day

In the field of happiness research, many experts agree joy and life satisfaction come from our ability to appreciate everyday events – the "little things" – that make up the majority of our lives: a fresh spring rain, the laughter of children, a perfect cup of coffee.

Much of this book has guided you to explore cherished memories – from monumental events such as birth and marriage to more commonplace details like types of transportation and hobbies.

While it can be pleasant to linger in yesterday's world, it's important to remember that some of our most treasured moments occurred on perfectly ordinary days – like today.

So ask yourself: How will I create new memories by making today meaningful, fun or significant? What can I do right now to focus my appreciation on the people, places and things surrounding me?

126

The first person I greeted today was:

_____

Currently, my favorite expression is:

_____

_____

If I changed one thing for the better in my daily routine, it would be this:

_____

_____

_____

My favorite time of day is usually: _____

because: _____

_____

_____

I'm looking forward to these three things today:

1 _____

_____

2 _____

_____

3 _____

_____

I promise...

Starting now, I promise to spend time doing something I enjoy – every single day.

That thing is: _____

_____

Signed, _____ _____ **Make today count.**

(your signature)   (date)